Ian Costabile

Who Stole my Cake?

Who Stole my Cake? is an original story, first published in Portuguese as "Quem Roubou meu Bolo?".

Translated by the author and Heather Day.

© 2016, 2017 Ian Costabile
Published by ArtLyra Press, Liverpool
All rights reserved. Published 2017.
www.artlyra.com

ISBN-13: 978-1-999749729

Cover by Natan Heber
www.natanheber.com
Illustrations by Noémie Lanos
www.noemielanos.wordpress.com

INTRODUCTION

I never eat warm cake, because my mum says it's better to wait for it to cool down. I went to my bedroom to wait but when I came back to the kitchen, my cake was gone! So, I asked myself in four different ways:

"Who stole my cake?"

"Who has stolen my cake?"

"Who took my cake?"

"Where has my cake gone?"

How is this story going to end? Can you help me to find out who has stolen my cake? Yes? So turn the page...

I
A Gorilla

A very strong gorilla wanted to be the strongest of all. Gorillas are already strong by nature, but this one, he was huge, like a mountain. In the morning, he used to lift tree trunks, in the afternoon, he used to throw rocks into the river and, at night, he used to crack nuts open with his fingers.

One day, he broke a cacao pod and, for the first time in his life, he tasted chocolate. It was pleasure at first bite, and soon he discovered that chocolate gave him more energy to train.

When the cacao season was over, he fled from the forest. He invaded the world of humans and his wild screams echoed through the city. In the language of the apes, he shouted: "Chocolate! Chocolate!"

Following his instincts, he discovered a delicious chocolate aroma. It was the scent of hot cake, which was coming from my window. Jumping from rooftop to rooftop, he came to my house, entered the kitchen and devoured the cake, the whole thing!

After that, he continued to eat chocolate and shared it with his friends. So, today, apes like chocolate more than bananas. Especially chocolate cake!

THE END
(NUMBER ONE)

II
Two Aliens

Zing and Zoing were on a mission to explore planet Earth but, when they arrived here, they just wanted to know about cakes! They had never tasted anything so yummy and soft. Apple, banana, carrot, chocolate, nut, ginger… there were so many flavours!

Zing and Zoing, disguised as humans, visited bakeries, grocery stores and sweet shops. However, they only knew how to point to a cake and say one thing: "This one, please!"

They were two very lazy extra-terrestrials because, although they had massive heads and superintelligent brains, they didn't want to learn the language of humans.

Thus, they travelled around the world, until they arrived in my country, in my city, in my home! When they saw that delicious chocolate cake, which my mum had made, they made themselves invisible, went to the kitchen, and stole my cake!

Afterwards, when they returned to their planet, those two aliens who had been so superskinny, became two fat aliens! They could barely get into their spaceship. Poor creatures…

THE END
(NUMBER TWO)

III
THE LOCH NESS MONSTER

The Loch Ness Monster, also known as Nessie, lives in Scotland. There, the Scots play a very noisy instrument, which the monster hates to hear, so he always hides inside a cave at the bottom of the loch, where he can rest in peace.

One day, he decided to travel through an underground tunnel that connects lakes and oceans.

He went through several countries, until one day he reached a very beautiful lake, near the garden of my house.

Sometimes, when it's summer, I swim in the lake. Imagine, I'm there in lake, swimming happily with my friends and all of a sudden, an enormous green monster pulls my foot! How scary is that?!

Well, continuing the story…

The monster arrived at the lake and when he lifted his head out of the water, he smelled the wonderful smell of cake. Of course he couldn't miss the opportunity to eat such a tasty treat from a distant land. So, without leaving the lake, Nessie stretched his long neck to my house, and passed it through the kitchen window. He got the cake in his mouth and while he withdrew his neck, a neighbour of mine who was passing by, saw the monster scene,

Nessie with a jaw full of cake. Of course she fainted on the spot!

After that, the monster was addicted to cakes, so tourists in Scotland need to beware. If you are visiting Loch Ness, be careful and don't take a cake, otherwise, the monster may appear and gobble it up!

THE END
(NUMBER THREE)

IV
PIRATES

Pirates of the past, swigging rum and raising the Jolly Roger, no longer exist. However, centuries ago, a cosmic ray hit a small pirate ship and immediately teleported it into the future. Yes, I think it's quite possible! A black hole could alter the space-time dimension and change the position of things, couldn't it?

The ship ended up on a beach, near my house. The pirates were very hungry, because time travel is very tiring and there is nothing to eat in mysterious time tunnels. They crossed many gardens, until they reached mine.

My neighbour looked at them and thought, "Since that new bar opened, on the corner, these drunkards keep coming into people's gardens to pee. They are so drunk that I can't even understand what they are saying." So, she decided to call the police.

The pirates broke down the door to my kitchen and came into the house. They had never seen so many strange things. They opened the fridge and began to touch everything. The milk, the eggs, the tomatoes, everything ended up on the floor.

They made a real mess! One curious pirate opened the dried food cupboard, and ended up eating raw pasta! The second curious pirate opened the spice cupboard, and ended up eating salt and pepper! The third curious opened the sauce and oils cupboard, and ended up drinking vinegar!

Finally, they found the chocolate cake, which was much more to their taste. They had just finished the cake, when the police arrived and took them all to jail. Anyway, they really enjoyed life in jail. Fights, free food, rebellions… and they took the opportunity to learn my language! Modern pirates are just like that.

THE END
(NUMBER FOUR)

V
My Sister

Yes, it was her! My sister, Tatiana. She loved eating cakes, of any size and any flavour. I wouldn't mind if she had eaten only a slice, but the whole cake? Come on!

It could only be revenge. When I was younger, I called her to play, but she didn't want to come because she wanted to have a bath with her dolls. While she was having a bath, I went to the garden and I caught lots of worms. I opened the bathroom door and, quickly, I threw them all into the bath, to see if they could swim. That day, I found out that worms can't swim and I also found out that my sister hates, really hates, worms!

So, when she saw that huge cake, she decided to take her revenge and eat it all herself. However, the cake was too big! It would be impossible to eat it all at once. So, she went to her bedroom and got several dolls, to help her to eat it. The doll called Gabrielle ate a slice. The doll called Isabelle, another slice. The doll called Danielle, another one. Chantelle also ate some… and Anabelle as well… Soon, every little damsel, with their names ending in 'elle', had eaten a slice.

However, dolls don't have real mouths, so, you can imagine the mess in the bedroom! There was chocolate everywhere. My mother almost left home. She said she'd put us in an orphanage. She also said, "I hope one day you will have children just like you, so you will learn your lesson!"

Then one day when she was a grown up, my sister had a son, who was just like her and, worst of all, he's mad about cakes!

THE END
(NUMBER FIVE)

VI
MOZART'S GHOST

Mozart, the famous composer, after his death, continued to make music in the spirit world. There, he met with other dead composers, some even crazier than him.

When he was alive, Mozart loved eating cakes. Cakes were the fuel that would give him energy to compose. The famous A Little Night

Music was composed after he ate a special apple and blackberry cake. Mozart wanted so much to eat a cake again, but, in the world of the spirits, there are no cakes, since ghosts cannot eat. So, he spoke with the ancient spirits and found a way to return to the world of the living, but for one day only!

In the world of the living, there was a lot of noise. The noise of city cars, horns, sirens, and the horrible music that modern people listened to. The future was, definitely, a musical nightmare for Mozart.

As soon as he got over the shock, he went on a quest for cake and when he'd almost given up, he saw through a window a huge and superdelicious cake, in a humble little house. Yeah, that's right, it was my house and my cake...

Mozart's ghost came through the wall, and, in his highly organised way, set the tablecloth and the cutlery on the table. He sat, and cut the first slice. With a lot of class, he ate slowly, savouring every bite. When he had finished, several ideas came into his head, and he began to write a beautiful composition, on a napkin. And so he composed his greatest work, Symphony no. 42, 'Earth', a composition full of passion for life and for our planet. Today, it's very much performed in the spirit world. If I had eaten the cake, maybe today I would have composed a great masterpiece… It's not fair!

THE END
(NUMBER SIX)

VII
AN ANT

Yes, an ant. Ants love sugar, therefore, they are always stealing cakes. And they are very lucky because they don't have teeth, so they can eat as much sugar as they please!

This little ant was passing by my kitchen and suddenly, he saw that beautiful chocolate cake. He thought, "I want to gobble up that cake! But how can I get it to my anthill?"

The first idea was to tie a rope around the cake and pull it. However, that didn't work, because although he was a strong ant, the cake was huge! So, he ate a little piece of the cake and returned to the anthill to ask his friends for help.

When he arrived at the anthill, he told two soldier ants that he had found the best cake in the world. However, they laughed at him and did not believe his story. Laughing, one of them said, "The little ant is a liar!" And the other one said: "I don't believe your tall story!" Luckily, ants have two stomachs, one to digest food and the other to take food to the queen. Therefore, he was able to give a piece of the cake to the soldiers so they could taste it. The soldiers were delighted by the sugariness of the cake, it was very good and very exotic! Then, they called together a group of a thousand soldiers to help carry the cake.

When the soldiers got inside the kitchen, Wagner's The Ride of the Valkyries started to play on the radio. The troop of soldiers went marching towards the cake, celebrating victory. The soldiers gathered around the cake, picked it up, and took it back to the anthill. However, they ate a lot of cake, so much cake in fact, they all got terrible diarrhoea. Poor little ants!

THE END
(NUMBER SEVEN)

VIII
A Little Princess

Once upon a time, there was a beautiful little princess, who lived in an enchanted land, where squirrels climbed happily on the trunks of colourful trees, rabbits danced to the sound of harps and dragons flew above infinite kingdoms.

When the princess was lying in bed about to sleep, her father, the king, told her the story of the chocolate mushrooms. Yes, chocolate mushrooms! The tale said that if a person ate a chocolate mushroom, this person would be transported to another world and that the only way to return would be by eating something else made of chocolate.

One day, she was running in the castle's garden, when she tripped on a rock. She took a tumble! When she opened her eyes, she saw that she was facing a chocolate mushroom that, in the sunlight, was melting slowly. All that delicious chocolate, dripping onto the grass… the temptation was too great and she couldn't resist, she had to try the mushroom!

And then, she slept. When she woke up, she was in a completely different world, where squirrels climbed grey tree trunks, rabbits danced to the sound of chaotic trumpets and dragons made of metal flew above a very strange village… Yes, this village was my city!

Walking along the streets, she found my house and saw my cake. She jumped through an open window, and tumbled into the kitchen. She went straight away to eat a little slice of the cake. Suddenly, everything began to spin and she returned to her own world, with the chocolate cake in her hands. She took a slice to the king and queen so they could try it, and of course they loved it! After that, they decided to look for more chocolate mushrooms, just to be able to eat more cakes like mine. Can you believe it?

THE END
(NUMBER EIGHT)

IX
A Hamster

Hamsters are funny animals. They are not ordinary rodents because they have almost no tail, use their cheeks to carry things, and have a scared-looking face. They are always involved in some kind of adventure, which never has an end. My neighbour has a hamster. His hamster loves to escape from his cage, to pick things up, mainly toilet paper. My friend's house always has lots of toilet paper all over the place.

My neighbour's hamster is called Coconut. He is as white as coconut. He, also, is extremely fast and big, very big. He has a massive bottom and when crawling, seems to be wearing a cloak, and as he also has a greyish beard, looks like a little wizard.

Last night, the hamster escaped, because he decided to go on the craziest adventure of his life. He decided to escape from my neighbour's house to explore mine. It was the summertime, and he knew that the bedroom window would be slightly open. So, he came up with a plan and calculated every single step that he would take.

When the clock chimed midnight, he knew that his owner would be asleep and it was time to act. His cage had no roof, so he climbed onto his water bottle, and using a toilet paper rope he'd made, climbed up. When he got to the top, he realised that he couldn't jump because it was too high. So, he crawled across the top of the cage until he came to a cushion. He jumped onto the cushion, and landed safely.

From there, he went to the bedroom window, which was slightly open, passed through the gap and jumped to the garden. He ran along the edges, fearing that a cat might see him. When he arrived at my house, he climbed the wall and jumped out of the window into the kitchen. When he saw that beautiful giant cake, he decided to steal it and take it to his home. He began eating the cake quickly, storing extra bits in his cheeks. However, it was too much cake, so his cheeks looked like two balloons. And, after that day, they stayed like that... forever. Serves him right, he dared to eat my cake!

THE END
(NUMBER NINE)

X
A PHILOSOPHER

Sitting under a tree, a philosopher thought. He thought, thought and thought. And while he was thinking, he came to think about shadows: "Shadows are images of figures that we know, but represented by the absence of light. Absence, because the light does not travel through opaque bodies. Therefore, most of the things that block light are shadow generators."

This philosopher is my neighbour. He always walks backwards and says complicated things about life. Today, he is focused on the subject of shadows, because shadows can represent concepts or ideas. He believes that ideas are more real than information we receive through our eyes.

In the backyard, he watched the sun draw shadows. He followed shadow after shadow. He found the shadow of an ant, of a flower, of a tree, of the clouds and, of course, himself. He followed the shadows until he arrived at my house and there, in the kitchen, was the shadow of... a cake!

He came closer, and he saw that the sun was shining on the cake and drawing its shadow. He decided to enter the kitchen. He stood in front of the cake, thinking, thinking and thinking. He had an idea: "If I eat this cake, I will have more energy and I will be able to stay philosophising for hours and hours!" But then he reconsidered: "The cake is not mine. It would be unethical to eat it." After reconsidering he thought: "This cake will have an end anyway. Everything in life has a beginning and an end, it is all a cycle."

And so, he entered into a long deliberation. To eat or not to eat, that is the question. Finally, he remembered that the Sun will not exist forever and, consequently, shadows will not exist forever. He concluded that he should not waste time asking silly questions, and decided to eat it. When he was finished, he stopped thinking of shadows and started to think about pleasure. The pleasure of eating such a soft and tasty cake. But could this chocolate cake also be, an illusion? That was the question that he would never be able to answer...

THE END
(NUMBER TEN)

XI
A Witch

A witch! When my mother was making the cake, she asked me to go to the neighbour's house to ask for a drop of vanilla essence. I didn't want to go, because everyone says that this neighbour is actually, a witch! However, I really wanted to eat this cake, so, I went and knocked on the door. No one answered, but through the window I saw some glass bottles on a table. One of them smelt like vanilla, so, I picked it up and I took it to my mum.

When the neighbour returned, she noticed that her magical bottle was gone. Yes, magical! She became desperate and started looking everywhere for it. You see, this bottle was very important, because it contained a magic potion of levitation. This means that what my mum put in the cake, was not vanilla!

The bottle wasn't in the house, so, the witch began looking for it in the garden. Suddenly, she looked at the floor and saw ants floating! She followed the trail of the floating ants, until she heard a cat meowing. It was her black cat, which was also floating. She continued following the path and saw that, in front of my house, other insects and animals were floating. The postman, who had come to deliver a letter, soon, was floating as well, about two meters above the ground, screaming in despair! It looked like a convention of yogis.

The witch ran into the kitchen of my house, saw the cake, and figured it all out. The warm cake was releasing the magic potion into the air, and all the creatures who breathed in this essence began to levitate.

Finally, the witch thought of throwing the cake away. But, that wouldn't work, because the cake would continue to release the magic potion. The only solution was to eat it. So, she ate the whole cake and as there was too much potion, not even she could withstand the potency of it. When she came out into the garden she began to float into the air. She floated up to the clouds and I think she only managed to return a week later. I'm glad I didn't eat the cake!

THE END
(NUMBER ELEVEN)

XII
A GUITARIST

In the basement of a noisy house lived a man who wore a headband and had long hair reaching down to his waist. There, he spent the day studying the most distorted musical scales on the planet.

This guitarist had a very special plectrum, which helped him to play faster and create extremely delightful solos. One day, after playing for hours and hours, he sat down to rest, and left his plectrum by the basement window. Suddenly, a seagull appeared at the window and, with its beak, seized the plectrum and flew away.

The guitarist, desperate, left the house, still holding his guitar under his arm, and ran towards the seagull. The gull flew further away, and the sunlight reflected the magical plectrum onto the clouds. Then, the gull landed on the roof of a house. The guitarist climbed onto the roof and, just as he was getting close to it, the naughty animal flew off once again! It flew near a fountain, in the middle of town and the guitarist began to attract everyone's attention. No one could understand why he was chasing a seagull.

Then, the seagull took flight again, flying upwards into the sky, crossing a rainbow. The guitarist didn't give up, and continued running after it, with a crowd of puzzled people following him.

Suddenly, the gull dropped the plectrum and it started to fall from the sky, through the clouds and was then caught in a whirlwind… Finally, it blew through the kitchen window, falling straight into my cake!!

Celebrating and finally happy, the guitarist climbed into my house through the window. But, the plectrum began to sink into sticky chocolatiness of the cake. The only way to find the plectrum now was to eat the cake. So, he stuck his hand in the cake and began to eat it. The cake was so good, that he ended up eating all of it, including his own plectrum! After that, he had a huge stomach ache…

THE END
(NUMBER TWELVE)

XIII
A Mad Scientist

Near my house, there is a secret laboratory. It's true, and it belongs to a quite an eccentric scientist, who works with a rather unusual chemical element: chocolate. When he was just a student, all the other scientists used to laugh at him. They thought his ideas were too crazy and ridiculous, and he would never realise his dreams. Because of this, when he graduated, he failed to get a job.

He began to make chocolate eggs, to sell at Easter Time, just to make some extra cash. He had fun doing this and soon, he learned how to model chocolate Easter bunnies. Next, he learned how to model chocolate birds. Then, he decided to invest all his money in a chocolate-modelling laboratory, inside his house.

After learning chocolate shaping techniques, he decided to be a little bit more ambitious and join his biotechnological knowledge with his chocolate shaping techniques and began to give life to his creatures or, perhaps, give life to chocolate!

However, the scientist wasn't happy. He wanted to take revenge on those who laughed at him in the past, so decided to create a gigantic chocolate monster, to destroy the whole city! So he prepared the ingredients, and began the production. The monster grew and grew... finally reaching a point where... there was no more chocolate to continue! Just a little bit more was needed to complete it, so the scientist ran out of his house to look for any kind of chocolate he could find. Soon, he found my house and saw the chocolate cake, through the kitchen window.

He took the cake and ran back to his lab. He threw it in a tube, and the process was complete. Soon, the laboratory was filled with flashing lights and the sound of sirens. Suddenly, a huge chocolate monster appeared, which burst through the roof of his house. The monster went walking through the city, lifting cars and throwing them at buildings and people. The police came and shot at the monster, but the bullets had no effect, they just disappeared into its gooey body. But, it wasn't long before the sun came up, and the chocolate monster began to melt! I think the scientist forgot that tiny detail: chocolate melts. Thank goodness!

THE END
(NUMBER THIRTEEN)

XIV
THE CRAZYMAN

Everyone called him crazy. He wore a hat, a yellow suit, black trousers and different coloured shoes (one was green and one was red). This man loved to eat banana skins, but hated bananas. His pet was a bat. In his house there were colourful rugs everywhere, including on the ceiling. He loved to listen to sustained chords and 'static music'. He talked with his different personalities and prayed every day to the great god of Greek mythology, Dionysus.

This man was passing through my city. He said that he had a sacred mystery to solve, and that the solution could only be found here. However, he didn't know exactly where to go. Suddenly, it began to thunder and, along with the darkness of the night, rain began to fall. The crazyman ran to the middle of the road, and began to dance, hoping that Dionysus would come to help him. Suddenly, he heard the voice of the god, directing him to the path of the sacred mystery.

On the way, he found a very tall man, whose name was Midas. This man said he had the power to turn anything into gold. Well, he wasn't crazy enough to fall for that! Of course, he didn't believe him. So, Midas touched the crazyman's hat, which immediately, turned to gold! Of course, the crazyman believed him then, and invited him to accompany him on his quest.

Meanwhile, back in my bedroom, I could hear a lovely song coming from the garden. The crazyman and Midas also heard it. It was a nymph, who was sat under the window of my kitchen, singing this beautiful melody. Delighted by the music, both men ran to her. The rain stopped and the garden transformed into a party. The three then began dancing in a circle. It was a clear night, lit by the constellation of Lyra. As he was dancing, the crazyman caught a glimpse of the cake in the kitchen and realised the secret was there! It could only be in that amazing cake.

He got the cake and took it to the garden. He put it on the floor, and they all sat around it. They stayed there staring at the cake, amazed and full of desire to eat it. Then, the deep voice of Dionysus came echoing from the stars: "Eat the sacred cake and come to the world of the gods." The crazyman then allowed Midas to grab the first slice. But as Midas touched the cake, it turned to gold! His friends disappeared, and the crazyman stood there, alone, with the golden cake in his hands. Today, he is very rich. Well, maybe he wasn't crazy after all?!

THE END
(NUMBER FOURTEEN)

XV
THE WRITER

Yeah! The writer of this book!

But, how can it be? The writer lives in the world of real people, how could he enter into my dimension and steal my cake? Well, let's investigate...

It all started when he had written a few chapters of this book, and he didn't know who else could steal the cake. A gorilla, Mozart's ghost, a guitarist... even the Loch Ness Monster had joined in the fun! So, while he was sleeping, he had a dream. A dream in which he helped to create world peace.

The writer is a person who believes in world peace, and that is because he loves all nationalities. He was born in Brazil, but his grandparents came from several different parts of the world; Italy, Germany, Spain and Lithuania... Besides, his name is Scottish, he lives in England and, also, he speaks Indonesian and French! He is not a citizen of one place, he is a citizen of the world, and, therefore, he is a defender of all nationalities! Including my own...

However, dreams are strange, and as he was thinking about world peace he started to think about other things that he loves... like delicious chocolate cake. Suddenly, influenced by his curious stories, he appeared in my country, in my city, in my house! He was dreaming about my cake... and, looking at my cake, there was no doubt, he had to eat it! Those are the rules of the book.

And so, he was caught in his own trap, and as you may have already guessed, the writer ate the whole cake. The writer or me? The writer and I are the same person, aren't they? Well, we are, but... we are not. It's a paradox. I get it! The paradox stole my cake! Hmm... no. Perhaps, it wasn't the writer. So who stole my cake, using his or her own imagination in all the stories of this book was it... the reader? Yes, it was you! Isn't that true, reader?

THE END
(NUMBER FIFTEEN)

www.ingramcontent.com/pod-product-compliance
Lightning Source LLC
Chambersburg PA
CBHW060540030426
42337CB00021B/4368